HAWAIIAN SONGS for UKULELE

Arranged by Chad

ISBN 978-1-4234-6727-4

HAL•LEONARD®
CORPORATION
7777 W. BLUEMOUND RD. P.O. BOX 13819 MILWAUKEE, WI 53213

Visit Hal Leonard Online at
www.halleonard.com

Aloha Oe

Words and Music by Queen Liliuokalani

vale. _____ Fare - well to

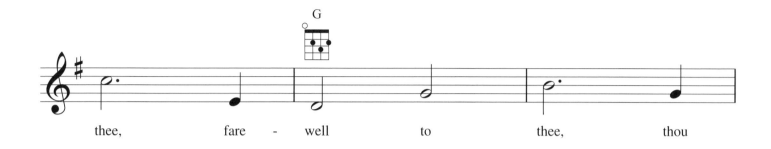

thee, fare - well to thee, thou

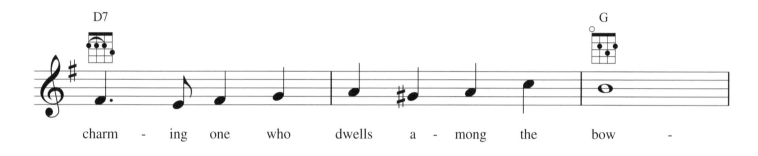

charm - ing one who dwells a - mong the bow -

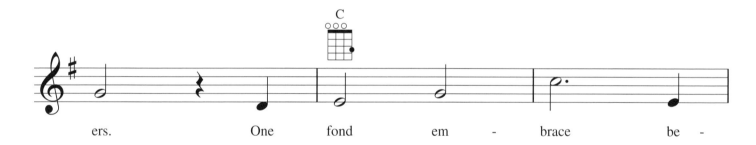

ers. One fond em - brace be -

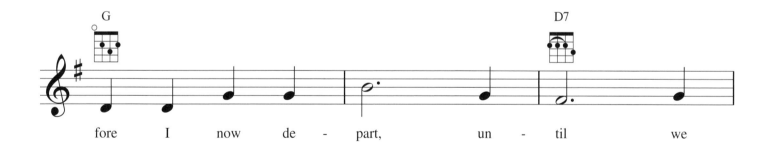

fore I now de - part, un - til we

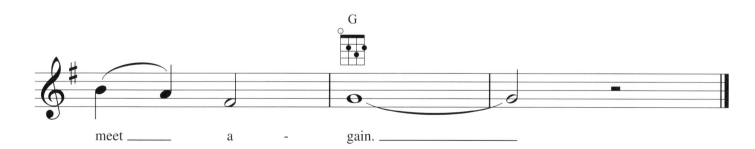

meet _____ a - gain. _____

Bali Ha'i

from SOUTH PACIFIC

Lyrics by Oscar Hammerstein II
Music by Richard Rodgers

First note

Most peo - ple live on a lone - ly is - land, _____
lost in the mid - dle of a fog - gy sea. _____
Most peo - ple long for an - oth - er is - land, _____
one where they know they would like to be. _____ Ba - li

Chorus

Ha'i may call you an - y night, an - y day. In your
Ha'i will whis - per on the wind of the sea: "Here am

Beyond the Rainbow

Words by Leon Pober
Music by Webley Edwards

Beyond the Reef

Words and Music by Jack Pitman

Bridge

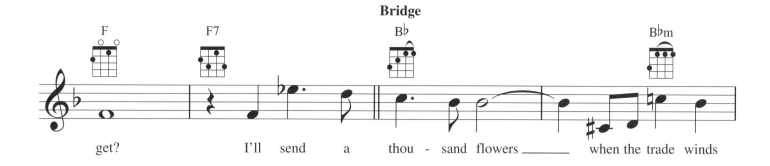

get?   I'll send a thou - sand flowers _____ when the trade winds

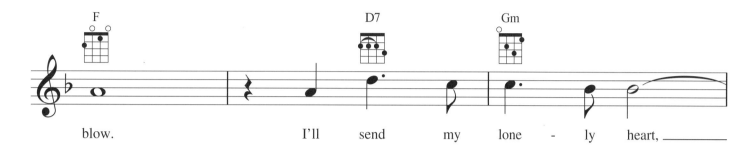

blow.   I'll send my lone - ly heart, _____

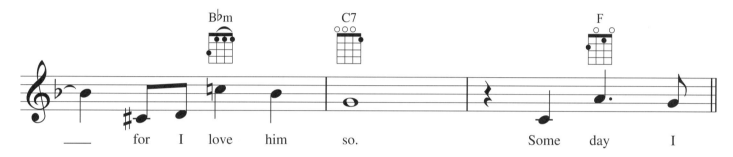

____ for I love him so.   Some day I

Verse

know _____ he'll come back a - gain to me. _____

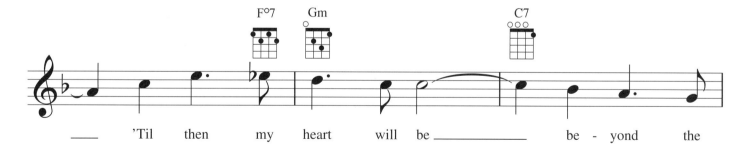

____ 'Til then my heart will be _____ be - yond the

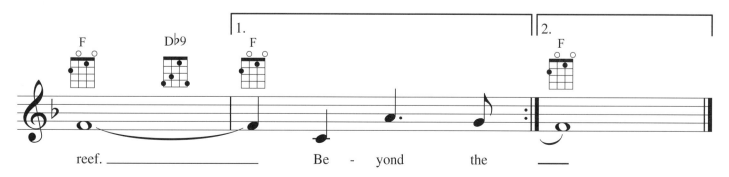

reef. _____ Be - yond the ____

9

Hanalei Moon

Words and Music by Bob Nelson

Harbor Lights

Words and Music by Jimmy Kennedy and Hugh Williams

Hawaiian Love Call

Written by Irmgard Aluli

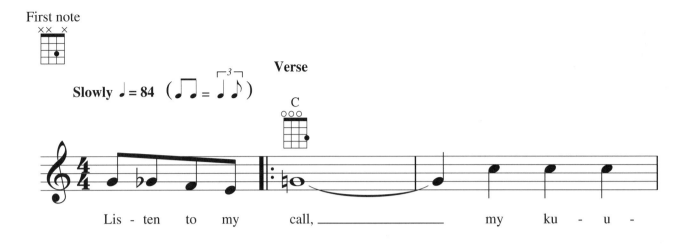

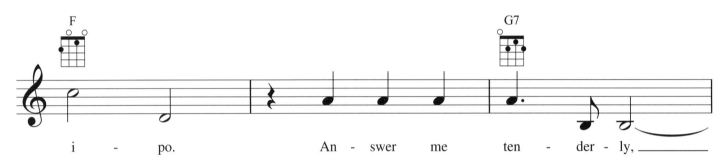

Lis - ten to my call, _____ my ku - u -

i - po. An - swer me ten - der - ly, _____

oh, so ten - der - ly. _____ Lis - ten to my

heart, _____ my ku - u - i - po,

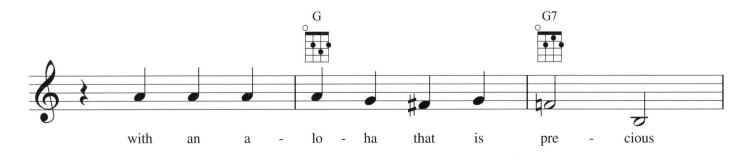

with an a - lo - ha that is pre - cious

sweet. _____ My dear - est one, _____

____ it's you I _____ want, my pre - cious

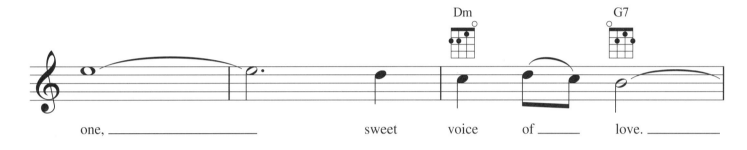

one, _____ sweet voice of _____ love. _____

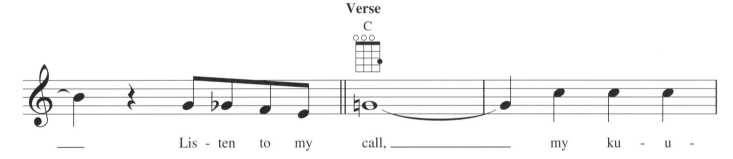

____ Lis - ten to my call, _____ my ku - u -

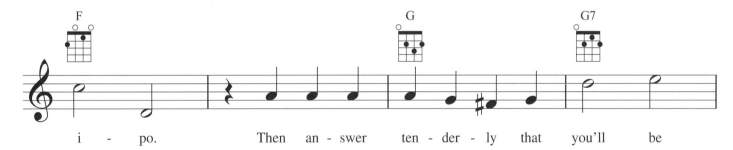

i - po. Then an - swer ten - der - ly that you'll be

mine. Lis - ten to my mine. _____

The Hawaiian Wedding Song
(Ke Kali Nei Au)

English Lyrics by Al Hoffman and Dick Manning
Hawaiian Lyrics and Music by Charles E. King

Here and now, dear, all my love I vow, dear.

Prom - ise me that you will leave me nev - er,

I will love you long - er than for - ev - er. _____

Bridge

Now that we are one, clouds won't hide the sun. Blue

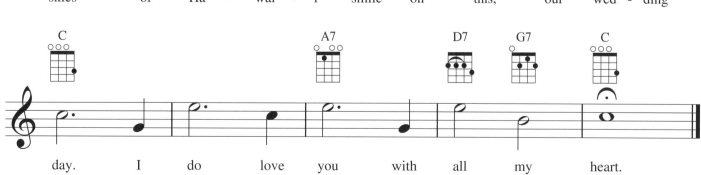

skies of Ha - wai - i smile on this, our wed - ding

day. I do love you with all my heart.

Ka-lu-a

Words by Anne Caldwell
Music by Jerome Kern

Kealoha (There Goes)

Words by Liko Johnston
Music by Liko Johnston and Howard Zuenger

dance that has that sway. When she glides a-cross the sand with a

smile up-on her face, she can steal an-y heart a - way.

Verse

Flow-ers bow their heads, the sun, and moon, and rain

all a-dore _____ Ke - a - lo - ha. She's a

beau-ty from those isles, she'll charm you with her smiles, that

danc-ing, ro-manc-ing, en-tranc-ing hu-la maid-en, _____ Ke - a -

1. lo - ha.

2. lo - ha. _____

Drifting and Dreaming
(Sweet Paradise)

Words by Haven Gillespie
Music by Egbert Van Alstyne, Erwin R. Schmidt and Loyal Curtis

Keep Your Eyes on the Hands

Words and Music by Tony Todaro and Mary Johnston

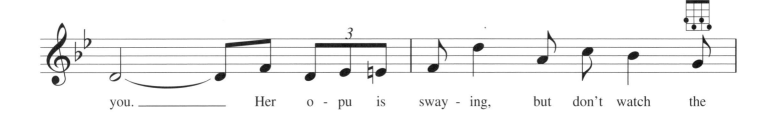

you. _____ Her o-pu is sway-ing, but don't watch the

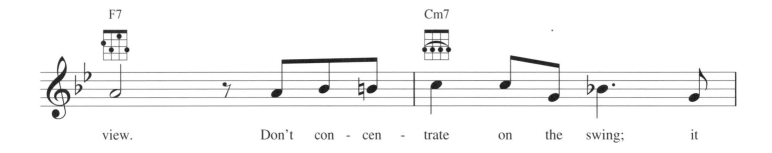

view. Don't con-cen-trate on the swing; it

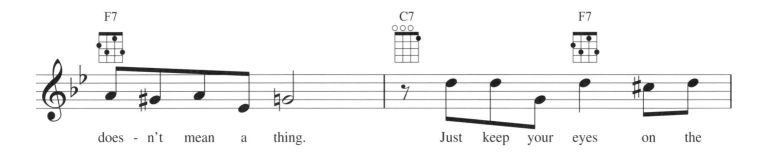

does-n't mean a thing. Just keep your eyes on the

Bridge

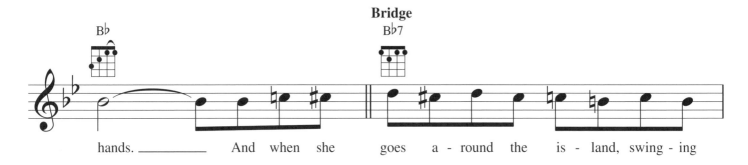

hands. _____ And when she goes a-round the is-land, swing-ing

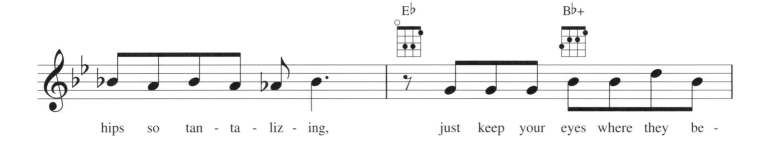

hips so tan-ta-liz-ing, just keep your eyes where they be-

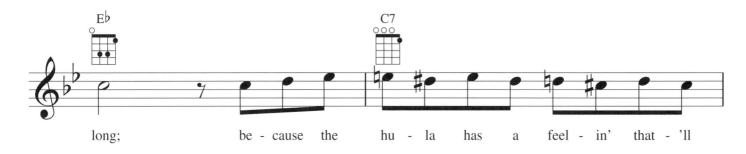

long; be-cause the hu-la has a feel-in' that-'ll

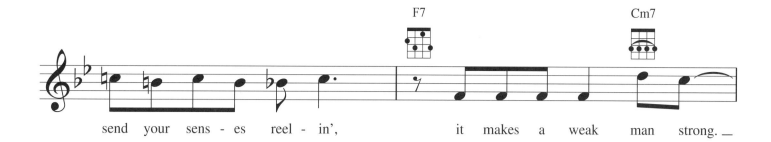

send your sens - es reel - in', it makes a weak man strong. —

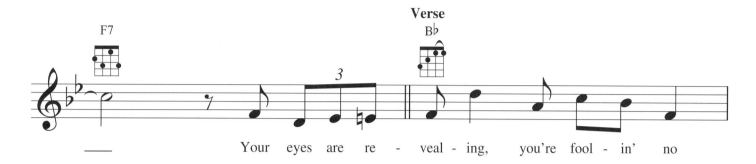

Verse

— ___ Your eyes are re - veal - ing, you're fool - in' no

one; _____ no use in con - ceal - ing we're hav - ing some

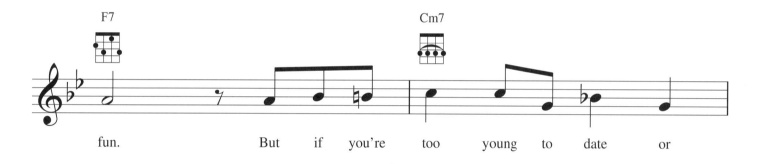

fun. But if you're too young to date or

o - ver nine - ty eight, just keep your eyes on the

hands. When - ev - er you're hands.

Lovely Hula Girl

Words and Music by Jack Pitman and Randy Oness

Mapuana

Words and Music by Lani Sang

Maui Waltz

Words and Music by Bob Nelson

Verse

I hear ___ the Mau - i waltz, my arms ___ are emp - ty now.

I hear ___ the Mau - i waltz, it does - n't

hurt some - how. You're here ___ with me when the

mu - sic starts to play. Play on, play

on ___ Mau - i waltz. ___ ___ Play

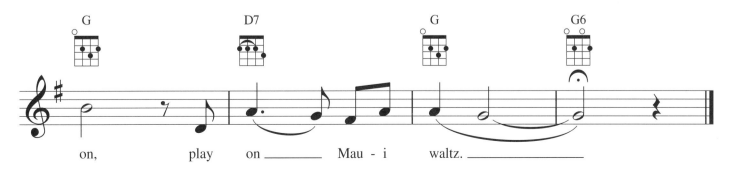

on, play on ___ Mau - i waltz. ___

Mele Kalikimaka

Words and Music by R. Alex Anderson

First note

Verse
Brightly ♩ = 104

F   B♭   F

Me - le   Ka - li - ki - ma - ka   is   the

thing   to   say _____ on   a   bright   Ha -

A♭°7   C7

wai - ian   Christ - mas   day. _____

Gm7   C7

That's   the   is - land   greet - ing   that   we   send   to   you ___

C+

___ from   the   land   where   palm   trees

sway. _____

Bridge

Here we know that Christ - mas will be green and bright. The sun will shine by day and all the stars at

Verse

night. Me - le Ka - li - ki - ma - ka is Ha - wai - i's way to say Mer - ry Christ - mas to you. _____

My Island Paradise

Words and Music by Webley Edwards, W.H. Miller and Leon Pober

First note

My is - land pa - ra - dise _____ a - cross the

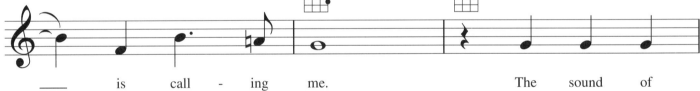

sea, _____ my is - land pa - ra - dise _____

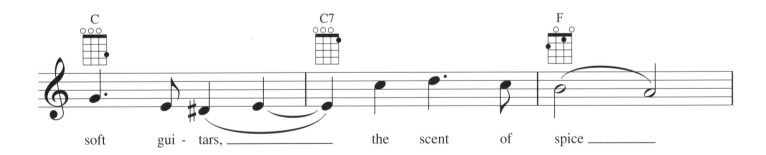

_____ is call - ing me. The sound of

soft gui - tars, _____ the scent of spice _____

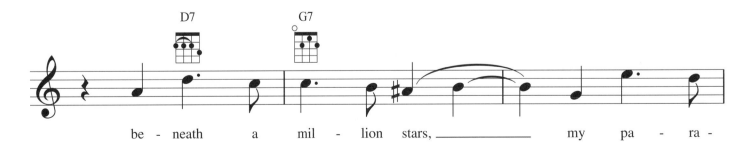

be - neath a mil - lion stars, _____ my pa - ra -

Now Is the Hour
(Maori Farewell Song)

Words and Music by Clement Scott, Maewa Kaithau and Dorothy Stewart

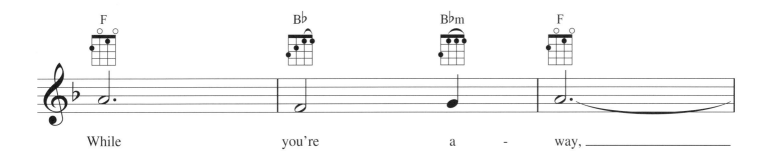

While you're a - way, _____

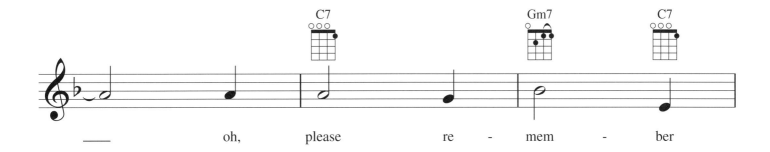

____ oh, please re - mem - ber me

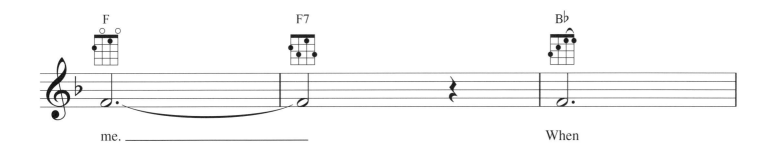

me. _____ When

you re - turn, you'll find me

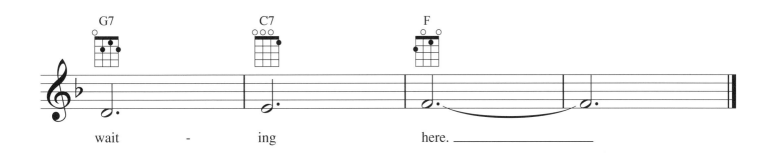

wait - ing here. _____

One More Aloha

Words and Music by Eddie Lund

One Paddle, Two Paddle

Words and Music by Kui Lee

Our Love and Aloha

Words and Music by Leolani Blaisdell

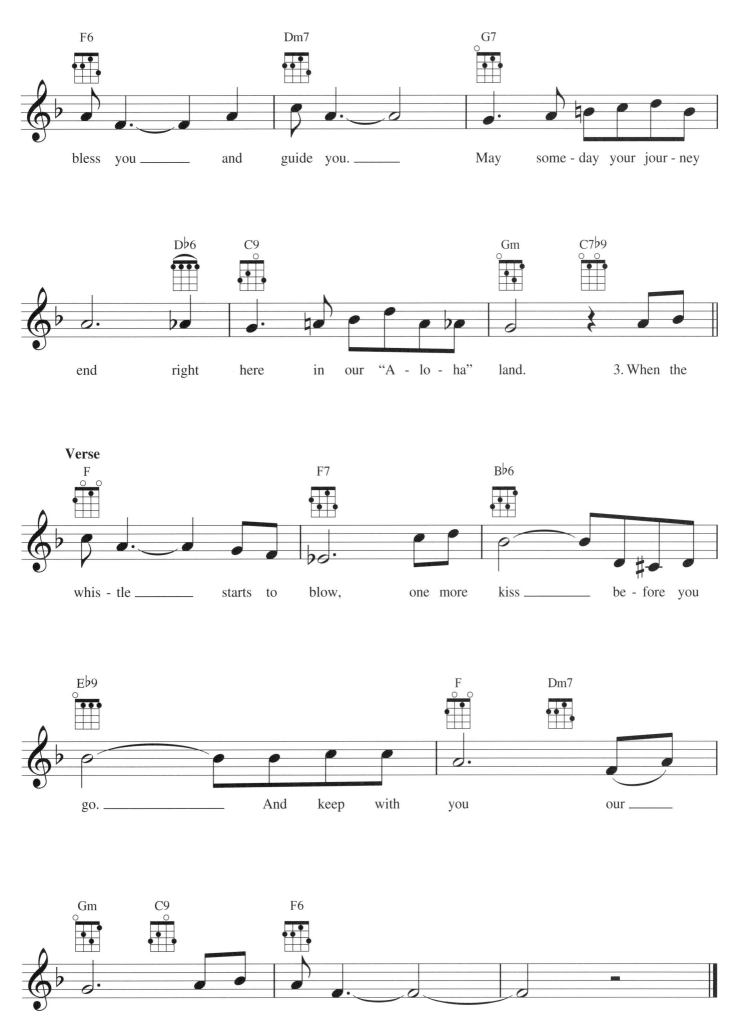

Pearly Shells
(Pupu O Ewa)

Words and Music by Webley Edwards and Leon Pober

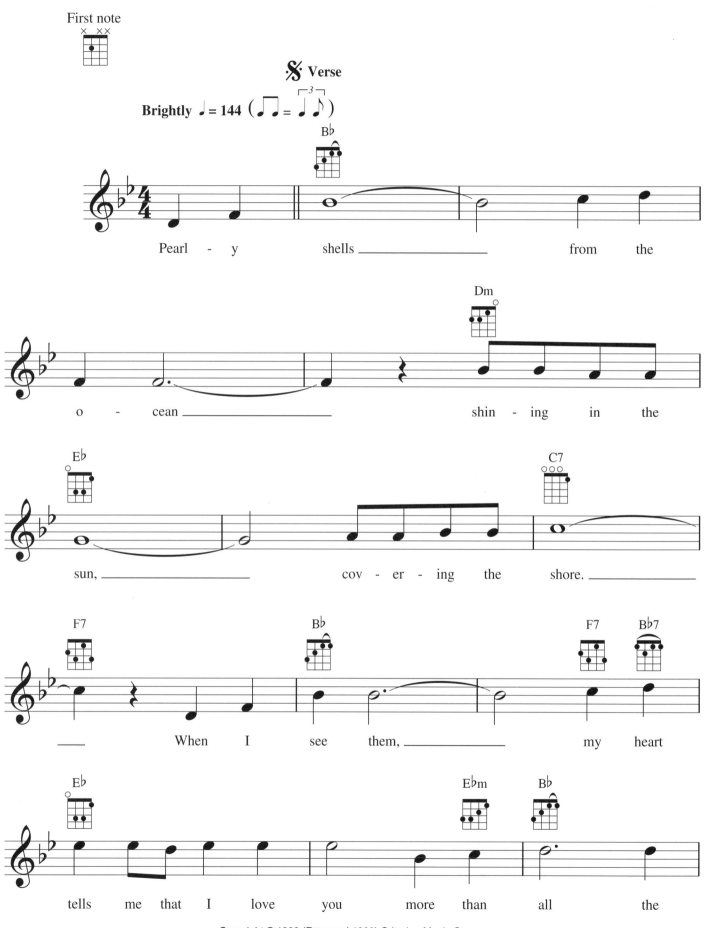

lit - tle pearl - y shells. For ev - 'ry

Bridge

grain of sand up - on the beach, I've

got a kiss for you; and I've got more left o - ver

D.S. al Coda

for each star that twin - kles in the blue. Pearl - y

Coda

shells. _____ More than all the

lit - tle pearl - y shells. _____

Quiet Village

Music by Les Baxter

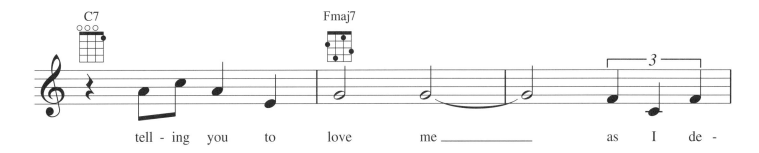

tell - ing you to love me _____ as I de -

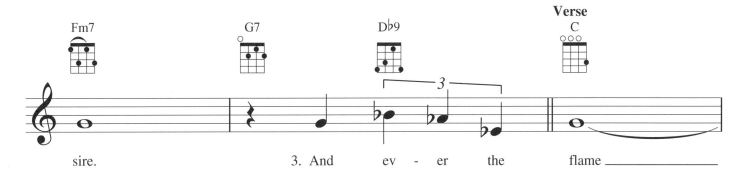

Verse

sire. 3. And ev - er the flame _____

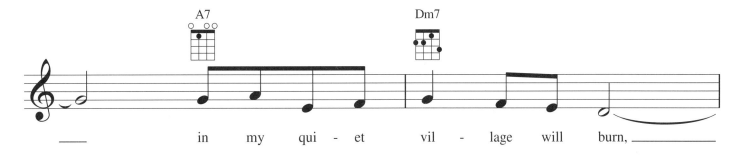

_____ in my qui - et vil - lage will burn, _____

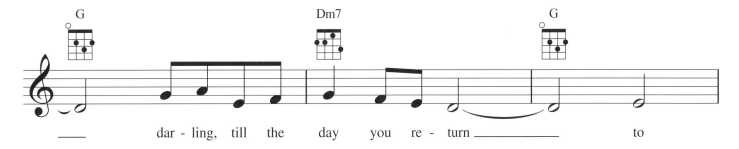

_____ dar - ling, till the day you re - turn _____ to

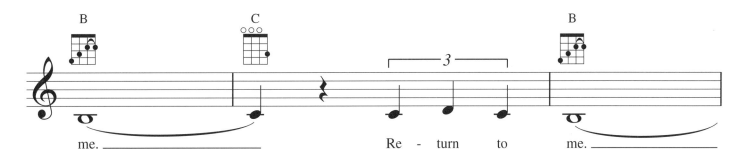

me. _____ Re - turn to me. _____

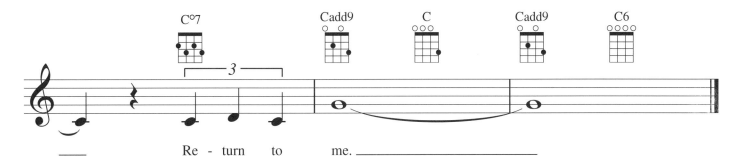

_____ Re - turn to me. _____

Red Sails in the Sunset

Words by Jimmy Kennedy
Music by Hugh Williams (Will Grosz)

Sands of Waikiki

Words and Music by Jack Pitman

sigh. _____ The old Ha - wai - ian

moon is rid - ing high. _____ My lone - ly heart is

cry - ing, "Here am I." _____

Bridge

Take me, make me yours a - lone, and let the fu - ture

be a - mong the gold - en sands of Wai - ki -

1. ki. For
2. ki. _____

The Moon of Manakoora

Lyric by Frank Loesser
Music by Alfred Newman

Sea Breeze

Words and Music by Al Hoffman, Dick Manning and Irmgard Aluli

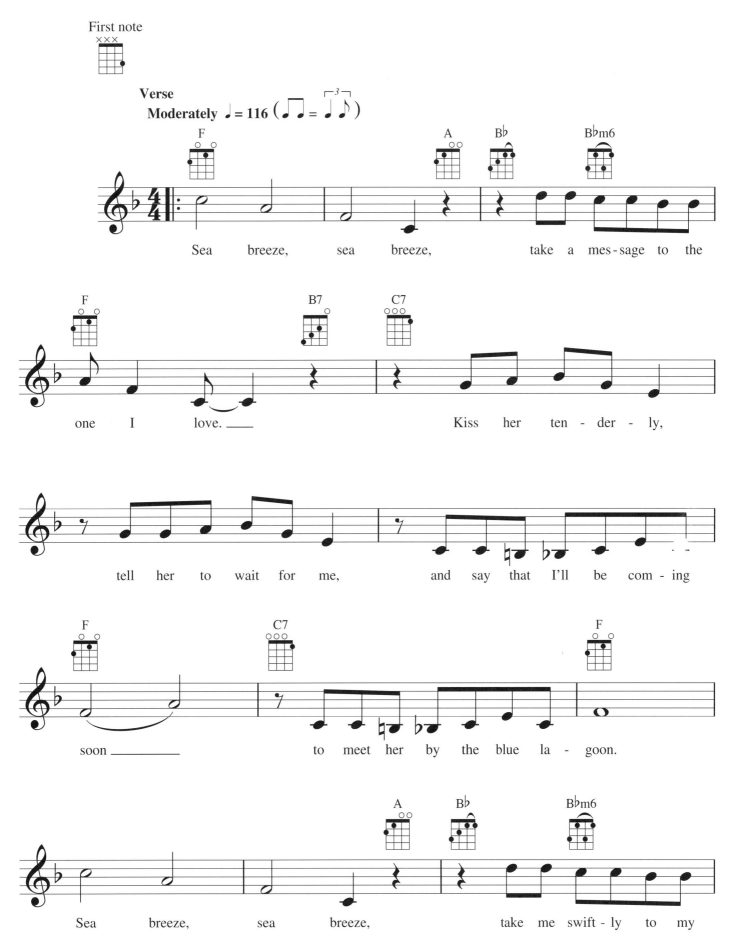

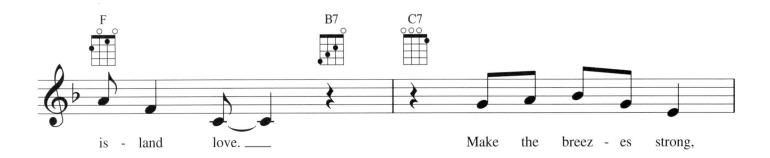

is - land love. _____ Make the breez - es strong,

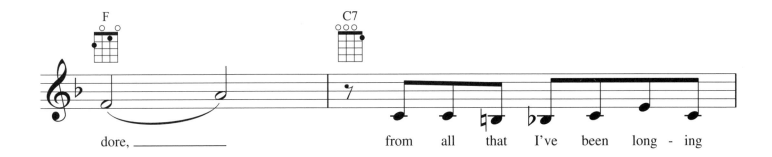

I've been a - way too long from lips and arms that I a -

dore, _____ from all that I've been long - ing

Bridge

for. Soothe her if you should find her

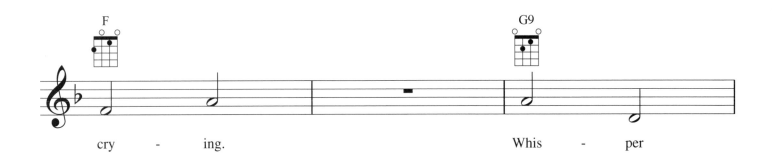

cry - ing. Whis - per

my love for her has been un-dy-ing.

Verse

Sea breeze, sea breeze, take a mes-sage to the

one I love. _____ Kiss her ten-der-ly,

tell her to wait for me, and say that I'll be com-ing

1.

soon _____ to meet her by the blue la-goon.

2.

goon. _____

Sleepy Lagoon

Words by Jack Lawrence
Music by Eric Coates

Sunny Days, Starry Nights

Words and Music by Leon Pober

Tiny Bubbles

Words and Music by Leon Pober

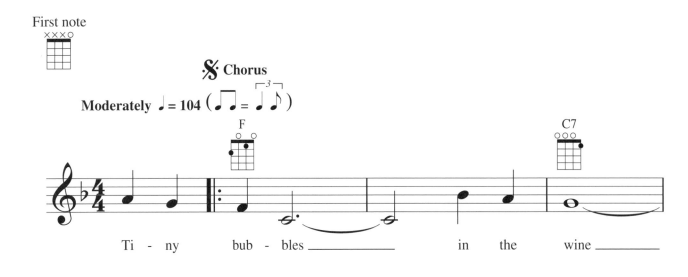

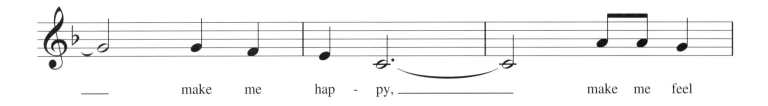

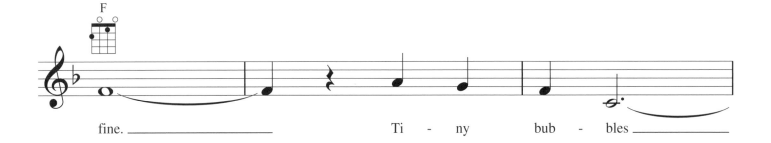

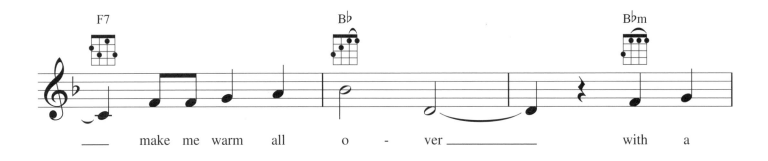

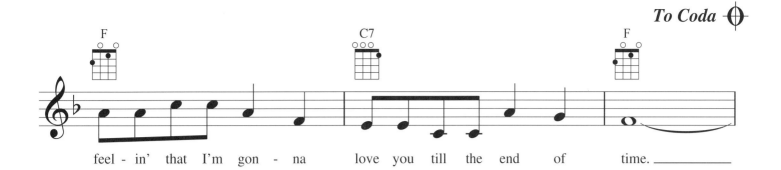

feel - in' that I'm gon - na   love you till the end   of   time. _____

Verse

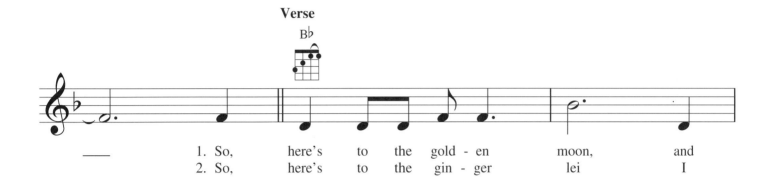

_____ 1. So,   here's   to   the   gold - en   moon,   and
       2. So,   here's   to   the   gin - ger   lei   I

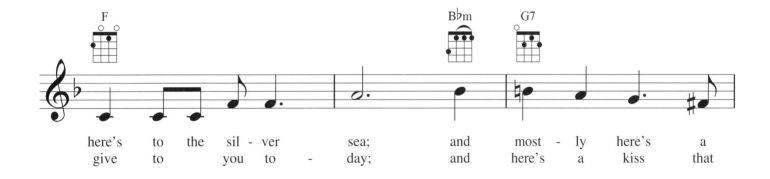

here's   to   the   sil - ver   sea;   and   most - ly   here's   a
give   to   you   to - day;   and   here's   a   kiss   that

2nd time, D.S. al Coda   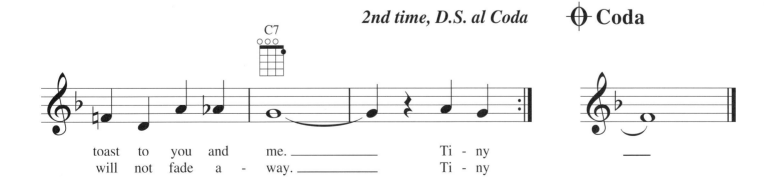 **Coda**

toast   to   you   and   me. _____   Ti - ny
will   not   fade   a - way. _____   Ti - ny

61

Waikiki

Words and Music by Andy Cummings

Song of the Islands

Words and Music by Charles E. King